Crispy Comforts

A Guide to Perfectly Fried Chicken and Grilled Vegetable Delights

While every precaution has been taken in the preparation of this book, the publisher assumes no responsibility for errors or omissions, or for damages resulting from the use of the information contained herein.

CRISPY COMFORTS

First edition. January 7, 2024.

ISBN: 979-8224417698

Written by Jose Maria.

Table of Contents

Jose Maria

❖ Introduction

A. Welcome and Brief Overview

Welcome to "Crispy Comforts: A Guide to Perfectly Fried Chicken and Grilled Vegetable Delights"! In this culinary journey, we'll explore the art of achieving perfectly fried chicken and the delightful flavors that come with grilling vegetables. Whether you're a seasoned home cook or a kitchen novice, this guide is crafted to elevate your comfort food experience.

A. The Art of Perfectly Fried Chicken

Indulge in the irresistible allure of perfectly fried chicken. Discover the secrets behind achieving that golden-brown, crispy exterior while maintaining juicy tenderness within. From selecting the finest cuts of chicken to mastering the breading techniques, we'll delve into the nuances that make fried chicken an art form.

A. Elevating Flavor with Grilled Vegetables

Dive into the world of grilled vegetable delights, where vibrant colors and smoky aromas take center stage. Learn the essentials of choosing the freshest produce, crafting tantalizing marinades, and mastering the grill for vegetables that are not only nutritious but bursting with flavor. Join us as we explore the perfect harmony between the crispy comforts of fried chicken and the wholesome goodness of grilled vegetables.

Chapter (1) Essential Ingredients and Equipment

A. Selecting the Best Chicken Cuts

When it comes to crafting the perfect fried chicken, the choice of chicken cuts is pivotal. Opt for a mix of thighs, drumsticks, and wings to cater to diverse preferences. The dark meat offers a juicy and flavorful experience, while wings provide the ideal canvas for crispy perfection. Ensure the chicken is fresh and free-range for the best results.

A. Flour, Seasonings, and Coating Options

Flour Mixture:

Combine 2 cups of all-purpose flour with 1 tablespoon each of paprika, garlic powder, and onion powder.

Season generously with salt and pepper to infuse flavor into every bite.

Marinade (Optional):

Enhance the flavor by marinating the chicken in buttermilk before dredging in the flour mixture.

Coating Alternatives:

Experiment with cornmeal, panko breadcrumbs, or a blend of both for unique textures and flavors.

A. Must-Have Kitchen Tools for Frying

Deep Fryer or Heavy-Duty Pot:

Ensure even cooking by using a deep fryer or a sturdy pot with enough oil to submerge the chicken pieces.

Candy or Oil Thermometer:

Maintain precise oil temperature, crucial for achieving that crispy exterior, using a thermometer.

Tongs or Slotted Spoon:

Flip and retrieve chicken pieces safely with long tongs or a slotted spoon.

Wire Rack:

Allow excess oil to drain off and keep the chicken crispy by placing it on a wire rack after frying.

A.   Choosing Fresh and Vibrant Vegetables for Grilling

Seasonal Variety:

Embrace seasonal produce for optimal freshness and flavor. Consider bell peppers, zucchini, mushrooms, and asparagus for a colorful and diverse vegetable medley.

Texture and Color Balance:

Mix and match vegetables with varying textures and colors to create a visually appealing and well-balanced grilled assortment.

Fresh Herbs:

Elevate grilled vegetables with fresh herbs like rosemary, thyme, or cilantro for added aroma and taste.

With these essential insights into ingredients and equipment, you're ready to embark on a journey towards creating the perfect fried chicken and grilled vegetable delights.

Chapter (2) Mastering the Perfect Fried Chicken

A. Preparing the Chicken: Brining and Marinating

Brining:
Ingredients:

- 1 gallon water
- 1 cup salt
- 1/2 cup sugar
- Whole peppercorns, bay leaves

Instructions:

- In a large container, dissolve salt and sugar in water.
- Add peppercorns and bay leaves.
- Submerge chicken pieces and refrigerate for at least 2 hours or overnight.
- Rinse and pat dry before proceeding.

Marinating (Optional):
Ingredients:

- 2 cups buttermilk
- 2 tablespoons hot sauce
- 1 teaspoon garlic powder

Instructions:

- Combine buttermilk, hot sauce, and garlic powder.
- Marinate chicken for at least 2 hours, enhancing tenderness and flavor.

A. Breading Techniques for Ultimate Crispy Texture

Dredging Process:

Coat chicken in seasoned flour, ensuring an even layer on all sides.

Double-Dipping (Optional):

For an extra crispy coating, dip the floured chicken back into the buttermilk, then dredge in flour again.

Resting Time:

Allow the breaded chicken to rest for 15-20 minutes. This helps the coating adhere better during frying.

A. The Right Oil and Temperature for Frying

Oil Selection:

Use a neutral oil with a high smoke point, such as vegetable or peanut oil.

Temperature Control:

Preheat oil to 350-375°F (175-190°C) for optimal frying. Maintain this temperature throughout the cooking process.

A. Achieving Golden Brown Perfection

Even Cooking:

Place chicken pieces in the hot oil, ensuring not to overcrowd the frying vessel for even cooking.

Cooking Time:

Fry until the internal temperature reaches 165°F (74°C) and the exterior is golden brown. Cooking times may vary based on the size of the chicken pieces.

A. Tips for a Healthier Fried Chicken Option

Baking Option:

Consider baking breaded chicken in the oven for a healthier alternative. Preheat to 400°F (200°C) and bake until internal temperature reaches 165°F (74°C).

Air Frying:

Utilize an air fryer for a crispy texture with significantly less oil.

Lean Cuts:

Opt for leaner cuts of chicken, like chicken breasts, to reduce overall fat content.

With these mastering techniques, your fried chicken will reach new heights of flavor and texture, providing a delightful culinary experience.

Chapter (2) Grilling Flavorful Vegetables

A. Seasonal Vegetable Selection

Bell Peppers:

Choose a mix of red, yellow, and green bell peppers for a vibrant color palette.

Zucchini:

Opt for small to medium-sized zucchinis, sliced into uniform rounds for even grilling.

Mushrooms:

Select firm and fresh mushrooms like cremini or button mushrooms.

Asparagus:

Pick thin asparagus spears for quicker and more even grilling.

Cherry Tomatoes:

Introduce bursts of sweetness with cherry tomatoes on skewers.

Red Onions:

Slice red onions into thick rings to add a hint of sweetness to the grill.

A. Marinades and Seasonings for Grilled Vegetables

Simple Herb Marinade:

Combine olive oil, minced garlic, fresh thyme, rosemary, salt, and pepper.

Citrus Garlic Marinade:

Mix olive oil, minced garlic, lemon zest, lemon juice, salt, and black pepper.

Balsamic Glaze:

Drizzle vegetables with a balsamic glaze made from balsamic vinegar, honey, and a pinch of salt.

Asian-Inspired Soy Glaze:

Create a soy glaze using soy sauce, sesame oil, ginger, and a touch of brown sugar.

A. Perfecting the Grill Marks

Preheating the Grill:

Ensure the grill is preheated to medium-high heat before adding vegetables.

Oil the Grates:

Brush the grill grates with oil to prevent sticking and achieve prominent grill marks.

Even Spacing:

Arrange vegetables evenly on the grill, allowing each piece to make direct contact with the grates.

Avoid Overcrowding:

Give vegetables ample space to cook evenly without overcrowding the grill.

A. Timing and Temperature for Optimal Grilling

Asparagus and Mushrooms:

Grill for 4-6 minutes, turning occasionally until tender with a slight char.

Bell Peppers and Zucchini:

Grill for 6-8 minutes, flipping halfway through, until they develop grill marks and are tender-crisp.

Cherry Tomatoes and Red Onions:

Skewer cherry tomatoes and red onion rings, grill for 3-4 minutes until tomatoes blister and onions caramelize.

Temperature Check:

Use a fork or skewer to check the tenderness of vegetables. They should be tender but not mushy.

With these tips, you'll be able to create a symphony of grilled vegetable flavors, each piece boasting the perfect balance of smokiness and tenderness.

Chapter (3) Complementary Sides and Dips

A. Classic Coleslaw with a Twist

Ingredients:

- 4 cups shredded green cabbage
- 1 cup shredded purple cabbage
- 1 cup grated carrots
- 1/2 cup mayonnaise
- 2 tablespoons Dijon mustard
- 2 tablespoons apple cider vinegar
- 1 tablespoon honey
- Salt and pepper to taste
- Chopped fresh parsley for garnish

Instructions:

- In a large bowl, combine green cabbage, purple cabbage, and grated carrots.
- In a separate bowl, whisk together mayonnaise, Dijon mustard, apple cider vinegar, honey, salt, and pepper.
- Pour the dressing over the cabbage mixture and toss until well-coated.
- Refrigerate for at least 30 minutes to let the flavors meld.
- Garnish with chopped parsley before serving.

A. Fluffy Mashed Potatoes

Ingredients:

- 4 large russet potatoes, peeled and diced
- 1/2 cup unsalted butter
- 1/2 cup warm milk
- Salt and pepper to taste
- Chopped chives for garnish

Instructions:

- Boil the diced potatoes until fork-tender.
- Drain and mash the potatoes while they are still hot.
- Incorporate butter and warm milk, continuing to mash until smooth.
- Season with salt and pepper to taste.
- Garnish with chopped chives before serving.

A. Tangy Dipping Sauces for Chicken

Honey Mustard Sauce:

- 1/4 cup Dijon mustard
- 2 tablespoons honey
- 1 tablespoon mayonnaise

Spicy BBQ Ranch Dip:

- 1/2 cup BBQ sauce
- 1/4 cup ranch dressing
- 1 teaspoon hot sauce (adjust to taste)

Instructions:

- For the Honey Mustard Sauce, whisk together Dijon mustard, honey, and mayonnaise.
- For the Spicy BBQ Ranch Dip, combine BBQ sauce, ranch

dressing, and hot sauce in a bowl.
- Serve these tangy sauces alongside your perfectly fried chicken for an extra flavor boost.

A. Fresh Salsas and Dips for Grilled Vegetables

Pico de Gallo:

- 2 cups diced tomatoes
- 1/2 cup diced red onion
- 1/4 cup chopped fresh cilantro
- 1 jalapeño, finely diced
- 2 tablespoons lime juice
- Salt and pepper to taste

Creamy Avocado Dip:

- 2 ripe avocados, mashed
- 1/4 cup Greek yogurt
- 1 clove garlic, minced
- 1 tablespoon lime juice
- Salt and pepper to taste

Instructions:

- For Pico de Gallo, mix tomatoes, red onion, cilantro, jalapeño, lime juice, salt, and pepper in a bowl.
- For the Creamy Avocado Dip, blend mashed avocados, Greek yogurt, minced garlic, lime juice, salt, and pepper until smooth.
- Serve these fresh salsas and dips alongside your grilled vegetables for a burst of flavor and texture.

Chapter (4) Creative Twists on Fried Chicken

A. Spicy Hot Chicken

Ingredients:

- 2 lbs chicken pieces (preferably thighs and drumsticks)
- 2 cups buttermilk
- 1 cup all-purpose flour
- 1 tablespoon cayenne pepper
- 1 tablespoon smoked paprika
- 1 teaspoon garlic powder
- Salt and pepper to taste
- Vegetable oil for frying
- Hot sauce for brushing

Instructions

- Marinate chicken in buttermilk for at least 2 hours.
- In a bowl, combine flour, cayenne pepper, smoked paprika, garlic powder, salt, and pepper.
- Dredge chicken in the seasoned flour mixture.
- Heat oil to 350°F (175°C) and fry chicken until golden brown and cooked through.
- Brush fried chicken with hot sauce for an extra kick.

A. Korean Fried Chicken

Ingredients:

- 2 lbs chicken wings
- 2 cups potato starch
- 1 cup soy sauce
- 1/2 cup gochujang (Korean red pepper paste)
- 1/4 cup rice vinegar
- 1/4 cup honey
- 2 tablespoons sesame oil
- 4 cloves garlic, minced
- 1 tablespoon ginger, grated
- Vegetable oil for frying
- Toasted sesame seeds and chopped green onions for garnish

Instructions:

- Coat chicken wings in potato starch and shake off excess.
- Fry the wings until golden brown and crispy.
- In a saucepan, combine soy sauce, gochujang, rice vinegar, honey, sesame oil, garlic, and ginger. Simmer until it thickens.
- Toss fried wings in the sauce until evenly coated.
- Garnish with toasted sesame seeds and chopped green onions.

A. Buttermilk and Herb-Infused Variations

Ingredients:

- 2 lbs chicken pieces (mix of your choice)
- 2 cups buttermilk
- 2 cups all-purpose flour
- 1 tablespoon dried thyme

- 1 tablespoon dried rosemary
- 1 tablespoon dried oregano
- Salt and pepper to taste
- Vegetable oil for frying

Instructions:

- Marinate chicken in buttermilk for at least 2 hours.
- In a bowl, combine flour, dried thyme, dried rosemary, dried oregano, salt, and pepper.
- Dredge chicken in the herb-infused flour mixture.
- Heat oil to 350°F (175°C) and fry until golden brown and cooked through.
- Serve with a side of herb-infused dipping sauce for an extra burst of flavor.

These creative twists on fried chicken will add a delicious variety to your culinary repertoire, bringing bold and unique flavors to your table.

Chapter (5) Pairing Fried Chicken and Grilled Vegetables

A. Creating a Balanced and Flavorful Plate

Colorful Array:

Arrange the golden-fried chicken pieces alongside vibrant grilled vegetables to create an appealing color palette on the plate.

Contrast in Texture:

Pair the crispy exterior of fried chicken with the smoky tenderness of grilled vegetables for a satisfying textural contrast.

Fresh Herbs:

Garnish the dish with freshly chopped herbs like parsley or cilantro to add a burst of freshness and elevate the overall presentation.

Sauce Drizzle:

Lightly drizzle a complementary sauce over the chicken and vegetables for an added layer of flavor and visual appeal.

A. Beverage Pairing Suggestions

Crisp White Wine:

A chilled Sauvignon Blanc or Pinot Grigio complements the fried chicken and grilled vegetables with its refreshing acidity.

Craft Beer:

Opt for a light and effervescent beer like a pilsner or a wheat beer to cut through the richness of the fried chicken.

Iced Tea:

A sweetened or unsweetened iced tea pairs well with the savory notes of the fried chicken and balances the smokiness of grilled vegetables.

Citrus Infused Water:

Create a refreshing citrus-infused water with lemon, lime, and mint to cleanse the palate between bites.

A. Presentation Tips for a Stunning Dish

Use Stylish Plating:

Choose elegant plating options like rustic wooden boards or sleek dinner plates to enhance the visual appeal of your dish.

Garnish with Edible Flowers:

Add a touch of sophistication by garnishing the plate with edible flowers for a pop of color and a hint of floral aroma.

Individual Servings:

Consider serving individual portions for a more polished presentation, allowing each element to shine.

Serving Sauces in Mini Bowls:

Present dipping sauces in small, aesthetically pleasing bowls on the side, allowing guests to customize their flavor experience.

Incorporate Unique Serving Utensils:

Use stylish tongs or serving utensils that complement the overall theme of your dish, adding a touch of finesse to the table.

By focusing on creating a visually appealing and harmonious plate, choosing complementary beverages, and paying attention to presentation details, you'll elevate your fried chicken and grilled vegetable feast to a stunning dining experience.

Chapter (6) Tips for Hosting a Fried Chicken Feast

A.   Planning and Preparation

Guest List Considerations:

Estimate the number of guests and tailor your fried chicken feast accordingly. Plan for a variety of chicken cuts and a generous assortment of grilled vegetables.

Make-Ahead Marinades:

Prepare marinades for both the chicken and vegetables a day in advance to save time on the day of the feast.

Fry in Batches:

Avoid overcrowding the frying vessel. Fry chicken in batches to ensure each piece achieves the perfect crispy texture.

Coordinate Cooking Times:

Plan your cooking schedule so that both fried chicken and grilled vegetables are ready to be served simultaneously, keeping everything hot and fresh.

A. Serving Ideas for Large Gatherings

Buffet Style:
Set up a buffet with different stations for fried chicken, grilled vegetables, and sides. This allows guests to customize their plates.

Family-Style Platters:
Arrange fried chicken and grilled vegetables on large platters for a communal dining experience, encouraging guests to share.

Outdoor Picnic:
Take advantage of outdoor spaces for a picnic-style feast, complete with blankets and casual seating.

Themed Decorations:
Enhance the atmosphere with thematic decorations, such as checkered tablecloths and rustic centerpieces, to complement the comfort food theme.

A. Storing Leftovers and Reheating Tips

Refrigeration:
Store leftover fried chicken and grilled vegetables separately in airtight containers in the refrigerator within two hours of serving.

Reheating Fried Chicken:
To maintain crispiness, reheat fried chicken in the oven at 375°F (190°C) for about 10-15 minutes. Avoid using the microwave, as it may result in sogginess.

Reviving Grilled Vegetables:
Gently reheat grilled vegetables in a skillet over medium heat, adding a splash of olive oil to refresh flavors and prevent drying out.

Serving Leftovers Creatively:
Transform leftovers into new dishes, such as shredded fried chicken tacos or grilled vegetable frittatas, to avoid monotony.

Freezing Considerations:

While fried chicken is best enjoyed fresh, grilled vegetables can be frozen and used in soups, stir-fries, or casseroles at a later date.

With these tips, you'll be well-equipped to host a memorable fried chicken feast, ensuring both the preparation and aftermath are seamless and enjoyable for you and your guests.

Chapter (7) International Flavors

A. Exploring Global Variations of Fried Chicken

Japanese Karaage:
Marinate bite-sized chicken pieces in a mixture of soy sauce, sake, ginger, and garlic. Coat in potato starch and deep-fry for a uniquely Japanese twist on fried chicken.

Southern-style Buttermilk Fried Chicken (USA):
Soak chicken in a tangy buttermilk marinade, seasoned with paprika, cayenne, and garlic. Dredge in seasoned flour before frying for a classic Southern flavor.

Indian Spiced Fried Chicken:
Infuse chicken with Indian spices like cumin, coriander, turmeric, and garam masala. Serve with a side of cooling raita for a delightful fusion.

Chinese Salt and Pepper Chicken:
Coat chicken pieces in a mixture of salt, white pepper, and a touch of five-spice powder. Deep-fry until golden brown for a simple yet flavorful Chinese-style fried chicken.

A. Incorporating Unique Spices and Marinades

Moroccan-inspired Chicken:
Marinate chicken in a blend of cumin, coriander, cinnamon, and lemon zest. Coat in a mix of chickpea flour and spices before frying for a North African-inspired delight.

Caribbean Jerk Chicken:

Infuse chicken with the bold flavors of a jerk marinade, featuring scallions, thyme, allspice, and Scotch bonnet peppers. Grill for a smoky Caribbean twist.

Mediterranean Herb-Infused Chicken:

Marinate chicken in olive oil, garlic, lemon juice, and a mix of Mediterranean herbs like oregano and rosemary. Coat in a blend of breadcrumbs and grated Parmesan before baking for a Mediterranean flair.

Thai Lemongrass Fried Chicken:

Create a marinade using lemongrass, fish sauce, garlic, and lime. Coat chicken in a light batter and deep-fry for a fragrant and crispy Thai-inspired dish.

A.   Fusion Ideas for Grilled Vegetables

Mexican Street Corn Salad:
Grill corn on the cob, then cut off the kernels and mix with mayonnaise, chili powder, lime juice, and crumbled cotija cheese for a zesty Mexican twist.

Italian Caprese Grilled Vegetables:
Grill tomatoes, zucchini, and eggplant, then layer with fresh mozzarella and basil. Drizzle with balsamic glaze for a Mediterranean-inspired side.

Japanese Miso-Glazed Eggplant:
Grill eggplant slices and brush with a glaze made of miso paste, soy sauce, mirin, and a touch of sugar for a sweet and savory Japanese fusion.

Middle Eastern Za'atar Roasted Vegetables:
Toss vegetables in olive oil and sprinkle with Za'atar spice blend before roasting for a flavorful Middle Eastern twist.

Explore these international flavors to add a global touch to your fried chicken and grilled vegetable repertoire, creating a culinary journey that spans continents.

Chapter (8) Healthy Alternatives

A.   Baked and Air-Fried Chicken Options

Baked Lemon Herb Chicken:
Marinate chicken in a mixture of lemon juice, olive oil, garlic, and fresh herbs. Bake in the oven until fully cooked for a lighter, oven-baked alternative.

Air-Fried Paprika Chicken Tenders:
Coat chicken tenders with a blend of paprika, garlic powder, and whole wheat breadcrumbs. Air-fry until golden and crispy for a healthier take on chicken tenders.

Yogurt-Marinated Baked Chicken:
Marinate chicken in Greek yogurt, cumin, and coriander. Bake until golden brown for a moist and flavorful baked chicken option.

A.   Lighter Coating and Seasoning Choices

Whole Wheat Flour Coating:
Substitute traditional flour with whole wheat flour for a heartier and healthier coating option for fried chicken.

Panko and Herb Crust:
Use panko breadcrumbs combined with dried herbs like thyme and rosemary for a lighter and crispier texture.

Spice-Infused Yogurt Dip:
Pair your chicken with a light and tangy yogurt dip infused with spices like cumin, paprika, and a hint of lemon.

A.   Grilled Vegetable Bowls for a Nutrient Boost

Quinoa and Grilled Veggie Bowl:

Grill a mix of colorful vegetables and serve over a bed of protein-rich quinoa. Drizzle with a light vinaigrette for a satisfying and nutritious bowl.

Mediterranean Chickpea Bowl:

Grill chickpeas alongside vegetables like cherry tomatoes, bell peppers, and zucchini. Toss with olive oil, feta cheese, and a sprinkle of oregano for a Mediterranean-inspired bowl.

Teriyaki Tofu and Vegetable Bowl:

Grill tofu and an assortment of vegetables, then toss with a homemade teriyaki sauce. Serve over brown rice for a protein-packed and wholesome bowl.

Rainbow Veggie and Hummus Bowl:

Grill a variety of colorful vegetables and arrange them in a bowl. Serve with a side of hummus for a nutrient-rich and satisfying meal.

A. Tips for Healthier Cooking

Use Lean Cuts of Chicken:

Opt for lean cuts like chicken breasts to reduce overall fat content.

Olive Oil Spray:

Use olive oil spray instead of submerging chicken in oil for a lighter coating.

Portion Control:

Serve smaller portions to encourage moderation and reduce calorie intake.

Increase Vegetable Intake:

Incorporate a variety of vegetables into both the grilled bowls and chicken preparations for added nutrients.

With these healthier alternatives, you can enjoy the comforting flavors of fried chicken and grilled vegetables without compromising on your commitment to a balanced and wholesome lifestyle.

Chapter (9) The Perfect Batter

A.   Experimenting with Different Batters

Classic Buttermilk Batter:
Combine buttermilk with flour, salt, pepper, and a touch of baking powder. Let the chicken soak for a few hours for a tender and flavorful result.

Beer Batter:
Create a light and airy batter using beer, flour, baking powder, and a pinch of salt. The carbonation in the beer adds a crispy texture to the fried chicken.

Tempura Batter:
Mix ice-cold water with flour and a bit of baking soda for a tempura-style batter. This results in an incredibly light and delicate coating.

Cornmeal and Cajun Spice Batter:
Combine cornmeal with Cajun spices for a Southern-inspired batter that adds a robust and flavorful crunch to your fried chicken.

A. Beer, Buttermilk, and Other Liquid Options

Beer:
The carbonation in beer creates a light and airy batter. Choose a beer with a mild flavor to avoid overpowering the taste of the chicken.

Buttermilk:
Buttermilk adds tanginess and tenderness to the chicken. It's a classic choice for a rich and flavorful batter.

Club Soda:
The effervescence in club soda makes the batter light and crispy. It's an excellent option for achieving a delicate coating.

Coconut Milk:
For a tropical twist, use coconut milk in the batter. It imparts a subtle sweetness and adds a unique flavor profile.

Yogurt:
Yogurt can create a thick and tangy batter. It's particularly suitable for a spiced or herbed coating.

A. Achieving Crispy Texture with Various Techniques

Double Dipping:
After the initial coating, dip the chicken back into the batter for a second layer. This technique adds an extra crispiness to the fried chicken.

Cornstarch Dusting:
Before dipping in the batter, lightly dust the chicken in cornstarch. This enhances the crispy texture and helps the batter adhere better.

Chilled Batter:
Keep the batter and chicken cold before frying. The contrast in temperatures helps create a crunchier exterior.

Frying Temperature:
Maintain the oil temperature between 350-375°F (175-190°C). Consistent high heat is crucial for achieving a crispy and golden-brown texture.

Resting Time:
Allow the battered chicken to rest for a few minutes before frying. This helps the batter adhere better during the frying process.

Experimenting with different batters, liquid options, and techniques will allow you to tailor your fried chicken to perfection, creating a delightful combination of flavors and textures.

Chapter (10) Vegetarian and Vegan Options

A. Plant-Based Chicken Alternatives

Crispy Tofu Nuggets:
Marinate tofu cubes in soy sauce, garlic powder, and nutritional yeast. Coat in a mix of cornstarch and breadcrumbs before baking or air-frying until golden and crispy.

Seitan Strips:
Use seitan strips as a meat substitute. Marinate in a flavorful blend of soy sauce, smoked paprika, and garlic powder before frying or grilling.

Chickpea Patties:
Create chickpea-based patties seasoned with cumin, coriander, and parsley. Pan-fry or bake until golden brown and serve as a delicious alternative.

Vegetarian Chicken Tenders:
Choose store-bought vegetarian chicken tenders or make your own using a blend of plant-based proteins. Coat in a seasoned batter and fry or bake for a meatless delight.

A. Tasty Fried and Grilled Vegetable Dishes

Cauliflower "Wings":
Coat cauliflower florets in a spicy buffalo sauce and bake until crispy. Serve with vegan ranch for a classic "wings" experience.

Portobello Mushroom Steaks:
Marinate portobello mushrooms in balsamic vinegar, garlic, and rosemary. Grill until tender for a hearty and savory meat alternative.

Grilled Stuffed Bell Peppers:

Fill bell peppers with a mixture of quinoa, black beans, corn, and spices. Grill until the peppers are tender, creating a flavorful and nutritious dish.

Eggplant Schnitzel:

Bread and pan-fry eggplant slices until golden brown. Serve with lemon wedges for a satisfying and plant-based schnitzel.

A. Vegan Sauces and Dips

Vegan Garlic Aioli:

Mix vegan mayonnaise with minced garlic, lemon juice, and a pinch of salt for a creamy and garlicky aioli.

Cashew Cheese Sauce:

Blend soaked cashews with nutritional yeast, garlic powder, and plant-based milk for a rich and cheesy sauce.

Spicy Vegan Sriracha Mayo:

Combine vegan mayo with sriracha sauce, lime juice, and a dash of agave syrup for a zesty and spicy dipping sauce.

Mango Avocado Salsa:

Dice mango and avocado, mix with red onion, cilantro, lime juice, and a pinch of salt for a refreshing and fruity salsa.

With these vegetarian and vegan options, you can create a diverse and delicious menu that caters to different dietary preferences, offering plant-based alternatives that are just as satisfying as their meat counterparts.

Chapter (11) Homemade Seasonings and Rubs

A. Crafting Signature Blends for Chicken

Classic Poultry Seasoning:

Combine dried sage, thyme, rosemary, marjoram, and a pinch of nutmeg for a timeless and versatile poultry seasoning.

Smoky BBQ Rub:

Blend smoked paprika, brown sugar, garlic powder, onion powder, and cayenne pepper for a smoky and sweet BBQ rub.

Lemon Herb Infusion:

Mix dried basil, oregano, parsley, and lemon zest for a bright and herbaceous seasoning perfect for grilled or fried chicken.

Spicy Cajun Blend:

Combine paprika, cayenne pepper, garlic powder, onion powder, thyme, and oregano for a bold and spicy Cajun seasoning.

A. Herb-Infused Rubs for Grilled Vegetables

Mediterranean Herb Mix:

Blend dried oregano, rosemary, thyme, and a touch of garlic powder for a Mediterranean-inspired rub for grilled vegetables.

Garlic and Herb Infusion:

Mix dried basil, parsley, garlic powder, and a hint of lemon zest for a versatile and aromatic herb rub.

Smoked Paprika and Cumin Rub:

Combine smoked paprika, ground cumin, coriander, and a pinch of cinnamon for a warm and smoky rub for grilled vegetables.

Lime and Chili Seasoning:

Blend chili powder, ground cumin, lime zest, and a touch of cayenne for a zesty and mildly spicy seasoning for grilled veggies.

A. Elevating Flavor Profiles with DIY Seasonings

Umami Bomb Seasoning:
Mix dried mushrooms, soy sauce powder, nutritional yeast, and garlic powder for a savory and umami-rich seasoning.

Maple Dijon Glaze Mix:
Combine dried mustard powder, onion powder, smoked paprika, and a touch of maple sugar for a sweet and tangy glaze mix.

Sesame Ginger Fusion:
Blend ground ginger, sesame seeds, soy sauce powder, and a dash of garlic powder for an Asian-inspired seasoning with a nutty and zesty kick.

Herb de Provence Twist:
Enhance traditional Herb de Provence with dried lavender, fennel seeds, and a touch of lemon zest for a fragrant and unique seasoning.

Experimenting with homemade seasonings and rubs allows you to tailor the flavors of your chicken and grilled vegetables to your liking, creating a signature culinary experience with each dish.

Chapter (12) Cooking for Crowds

A. Large-Batch Fried Chicken Recipes

Classic Southern Fried Chicken (Serves 20):
Use a mix of chicken pieces. Marinate in buttermilk and coat with a seasoned flour mixture. Fry in batches until golden brown. Serve hot for a classic crowd-pleaser.

Spicy Hot Chicken Bites (Serves 25):
Cut chicken into bite-sized pieces. Marinate in a spicy buttermilk blend and coat with a cayenne-infused flour mix. Fry until crispy and serve with cooling dips.

Herb-Infused Fried Chicken Tenders (Serves 30):
Choose chicken tenders for easy serving. Marinate in a blend of herbs and buttermilk. Coat with a seasoned flour mixture and fry until golden brown.

A. Grilling Vegetables for a Group

Rainbow Vegetable Skewers (Serves 20):
Skewer bell peppers, zucchini, cherry tomatoes, and red onions. Marinate in a simple olive oil, garlic, and herb mixture before grilling for a burst of colors and flavors.

Grilled Vegetable Platter (Serves 25):
Grill a mix of asparagus, mushrooms, bell peppers, and eggplant. Drizzle with balsamic glaze and sprinkle with fresh herbs for an elegant and delicious presentation.

Southwest Grilled Veggie Medley (Serves 30):
Toss corn, black beans, red onions, and bell peppers in a southwest-inspired spice blend. Grill until charred and serve as a flavorful side dish.

A. Tips for Efficient Cooking and Serving

Prep Ahead:
Marinate chicken and vegetables the night before to enhance flavor and reduce day-of prep time.

Fry in Batches:
Set up a dedicated frying station with multiple fryers to efficiently cook large batches of chicken.

Grill Stations:
If possible, set up multiple grilling stations to handle various vegetables simultaneously and speed up the cooking process.

Keep Warm:
Use chafing dishes or warming trays to keep fried chicken warm before serving.

Serve Buffet-Style:
Arrange the fried chicken and grilled vegetables on a buffet for easy access, allowing guests to serve themselves.

Coordinate Timings:
Plan cooking times carefully to ensure that both fried chicken and grilled vegetables are ready to be served at the same time.

Delegate Tasks:
If you have a team, assign specific tasks to individuals to streamline the cooking and serving process.

Quality Control:
Keep samples for quality control to ensure that the food maintains its optimal taste and texture.

By efficiently planning, preparing, and serving, you can successfully cook for crowds, ensuring that your fried chicken and grilled vegetables are hot, flavorful, and ready to be enjoyed by everyone.

Chapter (13) Leftover Transformations

A. Reinventing Fried Chicken and Vegetables

Chicken and Vegetable Stir-Fry:
Shred leftover fried chicken and chop grilled vegetables. Stir-fry with soy sauce, ginger, and garlic. Serve over rice or noodles for a quick and flavorful meal.

Fried Chicken Salad:
Slice cold fried chicken into strips and toss with mixed greens, cherry tomatoes, and a tangy vinaigrette for a refreshing salad.

Grilled Veggie Wrap:
Roll grilled vegetables in a tortilla with hummus or your favorite spread for a satisfying and portable lunch.

Chicken and Vegetable Quesadillas:
Layer shredded fried chicken and grilled vegetables between tortillas with cheese. Pan-toast until the cheese is melted for a delicious quesadilla.

A. Creative Ideas for Next-Day Meals

Fried Chicken Tacos:
Fill taco shells with shredded fried chicken, salsa, lettuce, and your favorite toppings for a tasty taco night.
Vegetarian Fried Rice:
Dice leftover grilled vegetables and mix with cooked rice, soy sauce, and sesame oil for a quick and easy vegetarian fried rice.
Chicken and Veggie Pizza:
Top a pizza crust with shredded fried chicken, grilled vegetables, and your favorite cheese for a flavorful homemade pizza.
Chicken and Vegetable Omelette:
Incorporate diced fried chicken and grilled vegetables into an omelette for a protein-packed breakfast or brunch option.

A. Reducing Food Waste with Inventive Recipes

Chicken and Veggie Frittata:
Whisk together eggs, add diced fried chicken and grilled vegetables, then bake for a hearty and nutritious frittata.

Fried Chicken Sliders:
Slice fried chicken into small pieces and sandwich between slider buns with your favorite toppings for a fun and bite-sized meal.
Veggie and Chicken Wrap:
Roll grilled vegetables and sliced fried chicken in a large tortilla with a spread of your choice for a satisfying wrap.
Chicken and Vegetable Soup:
Make a comforting soup by simmering fried chicken bones for broth and adding chopped grilled vegetables, creating a wholesome and flavorful meal.

A. Tips for Storage and Safety

Proper Refrigeration:
Store leftover fried chicken and grilled vegetables in airtight containers in the refrigerator within two hours of cooking.
Labeling:
Label containers with the date to keep track of leftovers and ensure freshness.
Reheating Safely:
Reheat fried chicken in the oven for crispiness and grilled vegetables on the stovetop to maintain their texture.

Transform Gradually:
Transform leftovers gradually to maintain variety and prevent monotony in meals.

With these inventive recipes, you can turn leftover fried chicken and grilled vegetables into exciting new dishes, minimizing food waste and maximizing the enjoyment of your home-cooked meals.

Chapter (14) Kitchen Hacks and Time-Saving Tips

A. Streamlining the Fried Chicken Process

Double Bagging for Coating:
Place the seasoned flour mixture in one bag and the wet ingredients (buttermilk, egg) in another. Double-bagging helps minimize mess and ensures an even coating.

Pre-Flouring:
Lightly coat chicken in flour before dipping it into the wet mixture. This helps the wet batter adhere better, resulting in a crispier texture.

Freezing for Crispiness:
Freeze breaded chicken pieces for 15-20 minutes before frying. This quick freeze helps the coating adhere and results in a crunchier texture.

Wire Rack Cooling:
After frying, place the chicken on a wire rack rather than paper towels. This prevents the underside from becoming soggy by allowing air to circulate.

A. Quick Grilling Techniques for Busy Days

Vegetable Skewers:
Thread vegetables onto skewers for faster grilling. This not only speeds up the cooking process but also ensures even cooking.

Pre-Marinating:
Marinate vegetables in a sealed bag in the refrigerator the night before grilling. This allows for a quick transfer to the grill when you're ready to cook.

Grill Baskets for Small Pieces:
Use a grill basket for small or delicate vegetables. It prevents them from falling through the grates and makes flipping them easier.

Pre-Grilling Protein:
Pre-cook protein (chicken, tofu) in the oven or stove before finishing on the grill. This reduces overall grilling time and ensures thorough cooking.

A. Clever Cooking Shortcuts and Tricks

Herb Ice Cubes:
Freeze fresh herbs in olive oil in ice cube trays. Pop out a cube when needed for an instant burst of flavor in your dishes.

Instant Marinade:
Use salad dressings as instant marinades. They not only add flavor but also contain oil that helps prevent sticking on the grill.

Blanching for Peeling:
Quickly blanch tomatoes or peaches in boiling water for 30 seconds, then transfer to an ice bath. The skins will easily peel off, saving time in the kitchen.

One-Pot Pasta:

Cook pasta in the same pot as the sauce. Add enough water to the sauce to cook the pasta directly, saving time on boiling a separate pot of water.

Pre-Chopped Ingredients:

Pre-chop and store common ingredients like onions, bell peppers, and garlic. Having them ready accelerates the cooking process when time is of the essence.

Cheat Sheet for Measurements:

Create a cheat sheet for common measurements and conversions. Tape it inside a cabinet door for quick reference while cooking.

Multi-Tasking Appliances:

Utilize multi-tasking appliances like Instant Pots and slow cookers to prepare ingredients while you focus on other tasks.

By incorporating these kitchen hacks and time-saving tips, you can make your cooking process more efficient, allowing you to enjoy delicious meals without spending excessive time in the kitchen.

Chapter (15) Gluten-Free Options

A. Gluten-Free Breading Alternatives

Almond Flour Coating:

Replace traditional flour with almond flour for a nutty and gluten-free alternative that adds a delightful flavor to your fried chicken.

Cornmeal Crunch:

Create a crispy coating by using cornmeal mixed with your favorite gluten-free seasonings. This adds a delightful crunch to your fried chicken.

Rice Flour Lightness:

Opt for rice flour for a light and airy coating. It creates a delicate texture that complements the natural flavors of the chicken.

Quinoa Crust:

Blend quinoa into a coarse powder for a nutritious and gluten-free crust that adds a unique texture to your fried chicken.

A. Celiac-Friendly Fried Chicken Recipes

Buttermilk Marinated Chicken (Gluten-Free):
Marinate chicken in gluten-free buttermilk with herbs and spices. Use a gluten-free flour alternative for the coating, ensuring a safe and flavorful fried chicken.

Crispy Cornmeal Chicken Tenders:
Coat chicken tenders in a mixture of cornmeal, gluten-free breadcrumbs, and seasonings for a flavorful and gluten-free twist on classic tenders.

Tapioca Starch Crunch:
Use tapioca starch as a coating for an extra crispy and gluten-free texture. Tapioca starch adds a light and airy quality to fried chicken.

Gluten-Free Fried Chicken Wings:
Prepare gluten-free chicken wings using a blend of rice flour, potato starch, and your favorite gluten-free seasonings. Fry until crispy and toss in your preferred gluten-free sauce.

A. Grilled Vegetables without Gluten Concerns

Lemon Herb Grilled Zucchini:
Marinate zucchini in olive oil, lemon juice, and a blend of gluten-free herbs before grilling for a light and refreshing side dish.

Garlic Rosemary Grilled Mushrooms:
Skewer mushrooms and marinate in garlic, rosemary, and olive oil before grilling for a savory and gluten-free vegetable option.

Cumin-Spiced Grilled Bell Peppers:
Toss bell peppers in a gluten-free mix of cumin, paprika, and olive oil before grilling for a smoky and flavorful side.

Gluten-Free Teriyaki Eggplant:
Grill eggplant slices and brush with a gluten-free teriyaki sauce made with tamari, ginger, and garlic for a sweet and savory twist.

A. Tips for Gluten-Free Cooking

Check Ingredient Labels:
Ensure that all seasonings, sauces, and pre-packaged items are labeled gluten-free.

Dedicated Cooking Utensils:
Use separate utensils and cookware for gluten-free items to avoid cross-contamination.

Gluten-Free Soy Sauce:
Substitute traditional soy sauce with gluten-free tamari or coconut aminos in your recipes.

Gluten-Free Baking Powder:
Choose a baking powder labeled as gluten-free to ensure the leavening agent in your recipes is safe for those with gluten concerns.

By incorporating these gluten-free options and tips, you can create delicious fried chicken and grilled vegetables that cater to individuals with gluten sensitivities or those following a gluten-free lifestyle.

Chapter (16) Childhood Favorites Reinvented

A. Nostalgic Flavors with a Grown-Up Twist

Truffle Oil Infused Mac 'n' Cheese:
Elevate classic macaroni and cheese by adding a touch of truffle oil for a sophisticated and flavorful twist.
Fancy Grilled Cheese:
Upgrade the classic grilled cheese sandwich by using artisanal bread, a variety of cheeses, and add-ins like caramelized onions or fig jam for a gourmet experience.
Grown-Up PB&J:
Use almond or cashew butter, fresh berries, and a drizzle of honey on whole grain bread for a more sophisticated take on the traditional peanut butter and jelly sandwich.
Caprese Chicken Tenders:
Coat chicken tenders in gluten-free breadcrumbs, top with mozzarella, cherry tomatoes, and basil before baking. Serve with a balsamic glaze for a kid-friendly Caprese twist.

A. Kid-Friendly Fried Chicken and Veggie Creations

Mini Chicken and Waffle Sliders:
Make bite-sized fried chicken pieces and sandwich them between mini waffles. Serve with a side of maple syrup for a fun and delicious meal.

Dippable Veggie Sticks:
Cut vegetables into stick shapes and serve with a variety of kid-friendly dips like hummus, yogurt-based ranch, or a mild salsa for a colorful and nutritious snack.

Cheesy Cauliflower Tots:
Transform cauliflower into cheesy tots by mixing with cheese, breadcrumbs, and seasoning. Bake until golden brown for a tasty and sneaky veggie treat.

Sweet Potato Fries with Cinnamon Dip:
Cut sweet potatoes into fries, toss with olive oil and cinnamon, then bake until crispy. Pair with a sweet yogurt and cinnamon dip for a delightful and healthier alternative.

A.   Getting Children Involved in the Cooking Process

Make-Your-Own Pizza Night:
Set up a pizza station with various toppings and let kids create their own personalized pizzas. This encourages creativity and a sense of ownership in their meal.

DIY Taco Bar:
Prepare a taco bar with different proteins, toppings, and tortillas. Kids can assemble their own tacos, fostering a sense of independence and enjoyment in the cooking process.

Decorate-Your-Own Cupcakes:
Bake cupcakes and provide an array of frostings, sprinkles, and toppings for kids to decorate their own cupcakes. It's a fun and delicious activity.

Smoothie Creations:
Set up a smoothie station with a variety of fruits, yogurt, and other add-ins. Let kids blend their own smoothie combinations for a healthy and interactive snack.

Homemade Popsicles:
Mix fruit juices, yogurt, or purees and freeze them in popsicle molds. Kids can create their own popsicle flavors with this simple and enjoyable activity.

Encouraging children to be part of the cooking process not only teaches them valuable skills but also makes mealtime a fun and interactive experience. With these reinvented childhood favorites, you can create meals that appeal to both the young and young at heart.

Chapter (17) Brunch Delights

A. Fried Chicken and Waffles

Classic Chicken and Buttermilk Waffles:
Serve crispy fried chicken over fluffy buttermilk waffles. Drizzle with maple syrup and sprinkle with chives for a sweet and savory brunch delight.

Spicy Honey Glazed Chicken and Cornbread Waffles:
Glaze fried chicken with a spicy honey mixture and serve on top of cornbread waffles. The combination of sweet, spicy, and savory flavors is a brunch sensation.

Savory Herb Waffles with Lemon Pepper Chicken:
Infuse waffle batter with herbs like thyme and rosemary. Top with lemon pepper fried chicken for a refreshing and aromatic brunch dish.

Buffalo Chicken and Blue Cheese Waffles:
Toss fried chicken in buffalo sauce and place it on waffles with crumbled blue cheese. Drizzle with ranch dressing for a brunch with a kick.

A. Grilled Vegetable Frittatas

Mediterranean Grilled Veggie Frittata:
Grill a mix of zucchini, cherry tomatoes, and bell peppers before incorporating them into a frittata with feta cheese and fresh herbs for a Mediterranean-inspired brunch.

Spinach and Mushroom Grilled Frittata:
Grill spinach and mushrooms before adding them to an egg mixture for a hearty and flavorful frittata. Top with grated Parmesan for a finishing touch.

Asparagus and Goat Cheese Frittata:
Grill asparagus until tender and combine with creamy goat cheese in a frittata. The result is a light and elegant brunch dish.

Sun-Dried Tomato and Basil Frittata with Grilled Veggies:
Add grilled vegetables, sun-dried tomatoes, and fresh basil to a frittata for a burst of vibrant flavors. Perfect for a colorful and delicious brunch.

A. Morning-Inspired Twists on Classic Dishes

Eggs Benedict with Fried Chicken:
Replace traditional ham with crispy fried chicken in Eggs Benedict. Top with poached eggs and hollandaise sauce for a decadent brunch twist.

French Toast Casserole with Grilled Peaches:
Make a French toast casserole with layers of bread, custard, and grilled peaches. Bake until golden brown for a delightful and easy brunch dish.

Breakfast BLT with Avocado Mayo:
Upgrade the classic BLT by adding a fried egg and a spread of avocado mayo. Serve on toasted bread for a hearty and satisfying brunch sandwich.

Shrimp and Grits with Grilled Asparagus:

Grill asparagus to add a smoky flavor to classic shrimp and grits. The combination of creamy grits, succulent shrimp, and grilled asparagus creates a brunch masterpiece.

With these brunch delights, you can create a memorable morning feast that combines the comforting elements of fried chicken, the freshness of grilled vegetables, and creative twists on classic breakfast dishes.

Chapter (18) Holiday Celebrations

A.   Festive Fried Chicken for Special Occasions

Rosemary and Cranberry Glazed Fried Chicken:
Glaze fried chicken with a combination of rosemary-infused honey and cranberry sauce for a festive and flavorful twist.
Pecan-Crusted Holiday Chicken:
Coat chicken in a pecan crust for a crunchy and nutty flavor. Serve with a cranberry dipping sauce for a festive touch.
Maple Glazed Apple Cider Fried Chicken:
Infuse fried chicken with the flavors of fall by using a maple and apple cider glaze. The sweet and tangy combination is perfect for holiday celebrations.
Herb-Butter Roasted Chicken with Sage Gravy:
Roast chicken with a generous herb butter rub and serve with a sage-infused gravy for a classic and comforting holiday meal.

A.   Grilled Vegetable Side Dishes for Holiday Feasts

Balsamic-Glazed Brussels Sprouts and Bacon Skewers:
Skewer Brussels sprouts and bacon, grill until crispy, and finish with a balsamic glaze for a savory and festive side dish.

Honey-Roasted Carrots and Parsnips:
Toss carrots and parsnips in honey and roast until caramelized. Sprinkle with fresh herbs for a sweet and herbaceous holiday side.

Cranberry and Pecan Stuffed Acorn Squash:
Grill acorn squash halves and fill with a mixture of cranberries, pecans, and cinnamon for a visually stunning and delicious side dish.

Garlic-Herb Grilled Potatoes with Rosemary Aioli:
Grill potato wedges with garlic and herbs and serve with a rosemary-infused aioli for a comforting and elegant holiday potato dish.

A.   Creating Memorable Culinary Experiences

Customized Holiday Buffet:
Set up a buffet with a variety of festive dishes, allowing guests to customize their plates and creating a memorable culinary experience.

Interactive Cooking Stations:
Incorporate interactive cooking stations like a carving station for roast chicken or a make-your-own grilled vegetable skewer station for a unique and engaging holiday celebration.

Festive Drink Pairings:
Pair holiday dishes with festive drinks like spiced apple cider, cranberry mimosas, or a rosemary-infused mocktail for a complete and memorable culinary experience.

Signature Holiday Desserts:

Create signature holiday desserts like a cranberry-orange trifle or a spiced pumpkin tiramisu to add a sweet finale to the celebration.

Holiday-Themed Decor:

Enhance the dining experience with holiday-themed decor, such as festive table settings, candles, and centerpieces, to create a warm and inviting atmosphere.

By infusing festive flavors into both fried chicken and grilled vegetable side dishes, you can elevate your holiday celebrations and create a memorable culinary experience for family and friends.

Chapter (19) Culinary Artistry

A. Edible Garnishes and Plating Techniques

Microgreens and Herb Sprinkles:

Garnish your dishes with microgreens or finely chopped herbs like parsley, cilantro, or chives to add a burst of freshness and color.

Citrus Zest:

Grate citrus zest (lemon, lime, or orange) over fried chicken or grilled vegetables to infuse a bright and aromatic flavor while enhancing visual appeal.

Edible Flowers:

Use edible flowers like nasturtiums, pansies, or violets to add an elegant and whimsical touch to your plated creations.

Fruit Salsa:

Create a vibrant fruit salsa with diced mango, pineapple, and berries. Spoon it over grilled vegetables for a sweet and tangy contrast.

A.   Elevating Aesthetics for a Stunning Presentation

Colorful Plating:
Arrange fried chicken and grilled vegetables on the plate with attention to color balance. Use a mix of vibrant vegetables and golden-brown chicken for an eye-catching presentation.

Height and Layers:
Create height on the plate by stacking or layering components. Place grilled vegetables on top of each other or lean fried chicken against a mound of mashed potatoes for visual interest.

Sauces as Art:
Drizzle sauces in artistic patterns on the plate. Use a squeeze bottle to create swirls, zigzags, or dots of colorful sauces for an elevated and visually appealing presentation.

Plate Framing:
Frame your dish by placing fried chicken at one end of the plate and grilled vegetables at the other, leaving the center open for a pop of color or a decorative element.

A. Turning Fried Chicken and Grilled Vegetables into Culinary Masterpieces

Deconstructed Chicken and Vegetable Stack:
Disassemble a piece of fried chicken, placing it alongside artfully arranged grilled vegetables. Drizzle with a complementary sauce for a deconstructed masterpiece.

Asian-Inspired Plating:
Arrange grilled vegetables in a geometric pattern, placing fried chicken on top. Garnish with sesame seeds and green onions, and drizzle with a soy-ginger glaze for an Asian-inspired culinary masterpiece.

Rustic Charm:
Present your dish in a rustic manner by serving grilled vegetables in a cast-iron skillet and fried chicken on a wooden board. Garnish with fresh herbs for a homey yet sophisticated touch.

Theatrical Smoke:
Infuse a hint of theatricality by using a smoking gun to add a subtle smoky aroma to grilled vegetables or placing fried chicken under a cloche for a dramatic reveal.

Artistic Sauces:
Experiment with artistic sauce designs. Create a swirl of balsamic reduction around the plate or use a spoon to make a zigzag pattern with a vibrant pesto for a touch of culinary artistry.

By incorporating edible garnishes, employing advanced plating techniques, and experimenting with artistic elements, you can transform fried chicken and grilled vegetables into culinary masterpieces that not only delight the taste buds but also captivate the eyes of those enjoying your creations.

Chapter (20) Behind the Scenes

A. Stories and Anecdotes from the Kitchen

The Secret Family Recipe:

Uncover the story behind a cherished family recipe for fried chicken or grilled vegetables. Share the tradition, memories, and the journey of passing down the culinary torch.

Kitchen Mishaps Turned Triumphs:

Laugh at the mishaps and unexpected surprises that occurred during the creation of your dishes. Sometimes, the most memorable moments come from unexpected kitchen adventures.

Cooking with Loved Ones:

Share heartwarming stories of cooking with friends and family. Highlight the joy and connection that comes from preparing and enjoying meals together.

The Culinary Discovery:

Narrate the tale of discovering a unique ingredient or cooking technique that transformed your fried chicken or grilled vegetables into something extraordinary.

A. Lessons Learned and Cooking Adventures

The Art of Patience:

Reflect on how patience plays a role in achieving the perfect crispiness of fried chicken or the ideal char on grilled vegetables. Explore the journey of learning to embrace the slow and deliberate process of cooking.

Mistakes as Culinary Teachers:

Share the valuable lessons learned from mistakes in the kitchen. Every burnt edge or over-seasoned dish contributes to the growth and refinement of your culinary skills.

Culinary Explorations:

Take your readers on a journey through culinary explorations, whether it's experimenting with exotic spices or mastering a new grilling technique. Share the excitement of broadening your culinary horizons.

Innovations in Home Cooking:

Explore the evolution of your home cooking style. Discuss the innovations, personal touches, and creative twists that have developed over time, turning ordinary dishes into signature creations.

A. Connecting with the Joy of Home Cooking

Creating Lasting Memories:
Recall instances when the aroma of fried chicken or the sizzle of vegetables on the grill filled the air, creating lasting memories with friends and family.

The Therapeutic Kitchen:
Reflect on how the kitchen serves as a therapeutic haven. Share stories of finding solace and joy in the simple acts of chopping, seasoning, and savoring the results.

Passing on Traditions:
Discuss the joy of passing on cooking traditions to the next generation. Whether it's teaching a family recipe or instilling a love for grilling, explore the meaningful connections created through these shared experiences.

Celebrating Culinary Heritage:
Embrace and celebrate the culinary heritage that has shaped your cooking style. Share anecdotes about the influence of cultural flavors and family traditions on your fried chicken and grilled vegetable creations.

By delving into the stories, lessons, and joyful moments behind the scenes of your kitchen, you create a personal connection with your readers. This chapter becomes an invitation to share not only recipes but the heart and soul that make your home cooking experiences truly special.

❖ Conclusion:

In the journey through "Crispy Comforts: A Guide to Perfectly Fried Chicken and Grilled Vegetable Delights," we've explored the artistry of home cooking, unraveling the secrets behind achieving the perfect crispiness of fried chicken and the delightful char of grilled vegetables. This culinary adventure has not only been about mastering techniques and flavors but also about creating a symphony of comfort and joy in your kitchen.

A. Celebrating the Joy of Home-Cooked Comfort:

Throughout this guide, the emphasis has been on the joy that comes from preparing and sharing home-cooked meals. From the nostalgia of childhood favorites to the sophistication of holiday feasts, each chapter has been a celebration of the comforting warmth that resonates from the heart of a well-prepared dish.

A. Encouragement to Experiment and Innovate:

Cooking is an ever-evolving art, and innovation lies at its core. In the spirit of experimentation, we've delved into creative twists on fried chicken, international flavor explorations, and healthy alternatives. The encouragement to innovate is an invitation to infuse your culinary creations with personal flair, making each dish uniquely yours.

As you continue your culinary journey, remember that the kitchen is a canvas for your creativity, a space where experimentation is not just welcomed but celebrated. Whether you're crafting a feast for loved ones or delighting in the process of mastering a new technique, find joy in the art of cooking.

Thank you for joining this exploration of crispy comforts. May your kitchen continue to be a source of inspiration, experimentation, and, above all, the joy of home-cooked comfort. Happy cooking!